Blood-Bought Promises of *Jesus*

Blood-Bought Promises of *Jesus*

A 30-Day, Personal Devotional

Robert & Debra Johnson

ISBN 978-0-9860180-0-8

Printed in the USA
Typesetting by www.wordzworth.com
Cover concept by Mike Ireland
Cover creation by www.wordzworth.com

www.bloodboughtpromises.com

We dedicate this book to God who has loved us more than we have loved ourselves and in His infinite wisdom chose to sacrifice his only Son for us while we were yet sinners and ignorant of our need for Salvation.

Also to our family who have been pillars for us over every mountain and through every valley. Thank you for your unconditional love, support and Godly wisdom.

CONTENTS

INTRODUCTION

"The cup of blessing which we bless, is it not the communion of the blood of Christ? The bread which we break, is it not the communion of the body of Christ?"
I Corinthians 10:16

Let us praise God that He loved us so much that He sacrificed His only begotten Son for the redemption of our sins and that we may live under the New Covenant!

The Old Covenant was divine words (laws) of God written in stone and used the blood sacrifice of animals. (Read Hebrews 8:7-9, and Hebrews 9:12-13.)

The New Covenant is through God's sacrifice of His Son, Jesus Christ. With Jesus' blood we have redemption of the transgression under the first covenant, and God writes His laws in our minds and hearts through the Holy Spirit. (Read Hebrews 8:10 and Hebrews 9:15.)

Jesus died on the cross and paid for our sins with his blood. Not only did His blood wash away our sins, but also promised us redemption, healing, forgiveness, protection, and so much more through our faith in Him.

This 30-day, personal devotional will help you better understand the power of the blood of Jesus, and gives you the opportunity to communicate intimately with Him.

To "ask and believe" in the blood, by faith in God's will.

Let us commune with Him.

God Bless.

DAY 1

NEW COVENANT THROUGH THE BLOOD

(Further reading: I Corinthians 11:24-25, Matthew 26:26-28)

"And He took the bread, gave thanks and broke it, and gave it to them saying, 'This is My body which is given for you; do this in remembrance of me.'

"Likewise He also took the cup after supper saying, 'This cup is the new covenant in My blood, which is shed for you.'" Luke 22:19-20

PRAYER

Father God, I thank you for the sacrifice of your Son, Jesus. I thank you that through His blood we were given a new covenant which promises access to God's best by faith.

In Jesus' name. Amen.

Personal Prayer

DAY 2

REDEMPTION THROUGH THE BLOOD

(Further reading: Colossians 1:13-14, Ephesians 1:7)

"Knowing that you were not redeemed with corruptible things, like silver or gold, from your aimless conduct received by tradition from your fathers;

"But with the precious blood of Christ, as of a lamb without blemish and without spot." I Peter 1:18-19

PRAYER

Father God, thank you for repairing my heart, redeeming me and restoring me to right fellowship with you, who is able to do exceedingly and abundantly more than I can think or ask.

I am blessed. In Jesus' name, Amen.

Personal Prayer

DAY 3

FORGIVENESS IN THE BLOOD

(Further reading: Colossians 1:14, Leviticus 4:20, Matthew 26:28, Ephesians 5:32)

"Whom God set forth as a propitiation by His blood, through faith, to demonstrate His righteousness, because in His forbearance God had passed over the sins that were previously committed." Romans 3:25

PRAYER

Father God, forgive me of my sins. Thank you for delivering me from evil doing and evil thoughts.

In Jesus' name, Amen.

Personal Prayer

DAY 4

THE BLOOD DELIVERS YOU FROM A GUILTY CONSCIENCE

(Further reading: 2 Corinthians 4:2, I John 1:7, Hebrews 10:22)

"How much more shall the blood of Christ, who through the eternal Spirit offered Himself without spot to God, cleanse your conscience from dead works to serve the living God?" Hebrews 9:14

PRAYER

Father God, thank you for deliverance from thoughts of guilt so that I can forgive myself to better serve you. I thank you for faith in your word in Hebrews 10:16-17, which promises that if I confess my sins and repent, my sins are forgiven and you remember them no more.

In Jesus' name, Amen.

Personal Prayer

DAY 5

THE BLOOD HEALS YOU

(Further reading: 3 John 2, Mark 5:34, Isaiah 53:5, Mark 5:24, Mark 9:23)

"Who Himself bore our sins in His own body on the tree, that we, having died to sins, might live for righteousness – by whose stripes you were healed." I Peter 2:24

PRAYER

Father God, thank you for allowing Jesus to bear all my infirmities. I rest in your word in 3 John 2, which says, "...that I prosper and be in health," and I declare by that I am healed by the blood of Jesus.

In Jesus' name, Amen.

Personal Prayer

DAY 6

THE BLOOD PROTECTS YOU

(Further reading: Jeremiah 32:27, Joshua 23:10)

"Now the blood shall be a sign for you on the houses where you are. And when I see the blood, I will pass over you; and the plague shall not be on you to destroy you when I strike the land of Egypt." Exodus 12:13

PRAYER

Father God, thank you for protecting me from all hurt or harm. Thank you for fighting all my battles. I know that greater is He that is in me, than he that is in the world. I will operate in faith and rebuke fear.

In Jesus' name, Amen.

Personal Prayer

DAY 7

PROSPERITY IN THE BLOOD

(Further reading: John 15:7, Psalm 37:4, Acts 20:32)

"He who did not spare His own Son, but delivered Him up for us all, how shall He not with Him also freely give us all things?" Romans 8:32

PRAYER

Father God, thank you for the blessing through the blood of Jesus. Thank you for blessing the works of my hands. Thank you for making me the head and not the tail, for making me above only, and not beneath. Thank you for making me a lender and not a borrower.

In Jesus' name, Amen.

Personal Prayer

DAY 8

THE BLOOD DELIVERS YOU FROM FEAR

(Further reading: 2 Timothy 1:7, I John 4:18, Romans 5:1-5, Isaiah 35:4, Psalm 31:24)

"As soon as Jesus heard the word that was spoken, He said to the ruler of the synagogue, 'Do not be afraid; only believe.'" Mark 5:36

PRAYER

Father God, thank you for freeing me from the spirit of fear. You did not give me a spirit of fear but a spirit of a sound mind. I take my authority through the blood of Jesus and bind every demonic attack on my thoughts.

In Jesus' name, Amen.

Personal Prayer

DAY 9

THE BLOOD SANCTIFIES YOU

(Further reading: Hebrews 13:12, Hebrews 10:16-17, Acts 26:18)

"By that will we have been sanctified through the offering of the body of Jesus Christ once and for all." Hebrews 10:10

PRAYER

Father God, thank you for sanctification through the blood of Jesus. Thank you for releasing me from the power of sin and setting me apart for God. Thank you for your mercy and grace. Thank you for the presence of the Holy Spirit to teach and guide me in living according to your word.

In Jesus' name, Amen.

Personal Prayer

DAY 10

THE BLOOD DESTROYS THE WORK OF THE DEVIL

(Further reading: Acts 26:17-18, Hebrews 2:14)

"He who sins is of the devil, for the devil has sinned from the beginning. For this purpose the Son of God was manifested, that He might destroy the works of the devil." I John 3:8

PRAYER

Father God, thank you for the blood of Jesus which destroys all the works of the devil. Thank you for the victory over sin, death and the grave by the blood of Jesus. I declare no weapon formed shall prosper against me- and I am more than a conqueror through Christ Jesus who strengthens me.

In Jesus' name, Amen.

Personal Prayer

DAY 11

THE BLOOD GIVES YOU PEACE

(Further reading: Colossians 1:20, Ephesians 2:14-15, Philippians 4:6 - 9)

"These things I have spoken to you that in Me you may have peace. In the world you will have tribulation; but be of good cheer, I have overcome the world." John 16:33

PRAYER

Father God, thank you for your peace, which surpasses all understanding, and thank you for the blood of Jesus that has overcome all tribulation. I declare by faith that I will be of good cheer and my hope is in Christ Jesus who guards my heart and mind.

In Jesus' name, Amen.

Personal Prayer

DAY 12

WE ARE JUSTIFIED BY THE BLOOD

(Further reading: Acts 13:39, Romans 3:23-24)

"But God demonstrates His own love toward us, in that while we were still sinners, Christ died for us.

"Much more then, having now been justified by His blood, we shall be saved from wrath through Him." Romans 5:8-9

PRAYER

Father God, thank you for loving me enough to allow Jesus to die for my sins, and be justified by grace through the redemption that is in Jesus Christ. I declare that I am justified by the blood of Jesus which always causes me to triumph.

In Jesus' name, Amen.

Personal Prayer

DAY 13

THE BLOOD RECONCILES YOU TO THE FATHER

(Further reading: 2 Corinthians 18-19, Romans 5:10)

"And you, who once were alienated and enemies in your mind by wicked works, yet now He has reconciled

"In the body of His flesh through death, to present you holy, and blameless, and above reproach in His sight." Colossians 1:21-22

PRAYER

Father God, thank you for making me blameless in your sight through the blood of Jesus. I declare that Jesus has reconciled me to you and that I am holy in your sight.

In Jesus' name, Amen.

Personal Prayer

DAY 14

THE BLOOD REDEEMS YOU FROM THE CURSE

(Further reading: Romans 6:14)

"Christ has redeemed us from the curse of the law, having become a curse for us (for it is written, 'Cursed is everyone who hangs on a tree'). Galatians 3:13

PRAYER

Father God, thank you for your grace through the blood of Jesus. Thank you for redeeming me from the curse, and allowing me to operate in the blessing. I declare that sin has no rule over me and I live under God's grace by faith.

In Jesus' name, Amen.

Personal Prayer

DAY 15

THE BLOOD BLESSES YOUR CHILDREN

(Further reading: Acts 2:38-39, Galatians 3:29)

"You are sons of the prophets, and of the covenant which God made with our fathers, saying to Abraham, 'And in your seed all the families of the earth shall be blessed.'"
Acts 3:25

PRAYER

Father God, thank you for my children, and thank you for the blessing over their lives through the blood of Jesus. I declare that they are heirs according to the promise and they are blessed in the name of Jesus.

In Jesus' name, Amen.

Personal Prayer

DAY 16

THE BLOOD GIVES YOU BOLDNESS

(Further reading: Hebrews 4:16)

"Therefore, brethren, having boldness to enter the Holiest by the blood of Jesus,

"By a new and living way which He consecrated for us, through the veil, that is, His flesh." Hebrews 10:19-20

PRAYER

Father God, thank you for the provision of boldness through the blood of Jesus. I thank you for access to your throne of grace where my help is obtained. I thank you for your mercy and for being a present help in a time of need.

In Jesus' name, Amen.

Personal Prayer

DAY 17

THE BLOOD RENEWS YOU

(Further reading: 2 Corinthians 4:16)

"And He died for us all, that those who live should live no longer for themselves, but for Him who died for them and rose again.

"Therefore, if anyone is in Christ, he is a new creation; old things have passed away; behold, all things have become new." 2 Corinthians 5:15 and 17

PRAYER

Father God, thank you for renewing your mercy every day and for restoring my strength when I feel tired. Thank you for making me a new creature through the blood of Jesus, and thank you for renewing my spirit.

In Jesus' name, Amen.

Personal Prayer

DAY 18

INTERCESSION THROUGH THE BLOOD

(Further reading: Romans 8:27, Hebrews 7:25, Isaiah 53:12, Isaiah 59:16)

"Likewise the Spirit also helps in our weaknesses. For we do not know what we should pray for as we ought, but the Spirit Himself makes intercession for us with groanings which cannot be uttered." Romans 8:26

PRAYER

Father God, thank you for your sacrifice of your Son for my sins. I know that because of His blood sacrifice, I now have an Intercessor who provides help in times of weakness and who acts on my behalf when I don't know what to say.

In Jesus' name, Amen.

Personal Prayer

DAY 19

THE BLOOD CLEANSES OUR SINS

(Further reading: I John 1:9, Revelation 1:5)

"But if we walk in the light as He is in the light, we have fellowship with one another, and the blood of Jesus Christ His Son cleanses us from all sin." I John 1:7

PRAYER

Father God, thank you for cleansing me of my sins and thank you for reconciliation through the blood of Jesus. I declare that because of the blood, I am made righteous in your sight by faith.

In Jesus' name, Amen.

Personal Prayer

DAY 20

THE BLOOD GIVES LIFE

(Further reading: John 6:57, John 10:10-11, John 10:27-28, Proverbs 19:23)

"Then Jesus said to them, 'Most assuredly, I say to you, unless you eat the flesh of the Son of Man and drink His blood, you have no life in you.'" John 6:53

PRAYER

Father God, thank you for access to abundant life by faith through the sacrificed body and blood of Jesus Christ. In John 10:10, Jesus said, "...I have come that they may have life and that they may have it more abundantly." I confess that I receive abundant life by faith through Christ Jesus.

In Jesus' name, Amen.

Personal Prayer

DAY 21

GRACE THROUGH FAITH IN THE BLOOD

(Further reading: John 1:16-17, Romans 16:20, John 1:14)

"Being justified freely by His grace through the redemption that is in Christ Jesus.

"Whom God set forth as a propitiation by His blood, through faith, to demonstrate His righteousness, because in His forbearance God had passed over the sins that were previously committed." Romans 3:24-25

PRAYER

Father God, thank you for your grace and redemption in Jesus Christ. Thank you for allowing me to receive out of your abundance. Through Christ you have supplied me with one grace after another, and spiritual blessings upon spiritual blessings, and favor upon favor, and gifts upon gifts.

In Jesus' name, Amen.

Personal Prayer

DAY 22

THE BLOOD HAS VICTORY OVER SATAN

(Further reading: Acts 26:18, Romans 16:20)

"And they overcame him by the blood of the Lamb and by the word of their testimony, and they did not love their lives to the death." Revelation 12:11

PRAYER

Father God, thank you for the blood of Jesus which gives me victory over Satan and always causes me to triumph. Thank you for the grace to allow my testimony to flow freely from my mouth and to declare victory in every area of my life by faith.

In Jesus' name, Amen.

Personal Prayer

DAY 23

THE BLOOD TURNS SORROW INTO JOY

(Further reading: Proverbs 10:22, Revelation 21:4, Isaiah 53:4-5, 2 Corinthians 7:10)

"Most assuredly, I say to you that you will weep and lament, but the world will rejoice; and you will be sorrowful, but your sorrow will be turned into joy." John 16:20

"Therefore you now have sorrow; but I will see you again and your heart will rejoice, and your joy no one will take from you." John 16:22

PRAYER

Father God, thank you for the blood of Jesus which promises to turn my sorrow into joy. Thank you for comforting me during times of grief and disappointment. I declare that any godly sorrow produces repentance and deliverance from evil and never brings regret, leading to salvation.

In Jesus' name, Amen.

Personal Prayer

DAY 24

THE BLOOD MAKES ATONEMENT FOR YOUR SOUL

(Further reading: Hebrews 9:22, Hebrews 9:18, Exodus 24:8, Luke 22:20, Romans 3:25)

"For the life of the flesh is in the blood, and I have given it to you upon the altar to make atonement for your souls; for it is the blood that makes atonement for the soul."
Leviticus 17:11

PRAYER

Father God, thank you for the sacrifice of your son Jesus Christ to atone my sins. Thank you for the blood that brings me into a right relationship with you by faith. Thank you for the blood that blots out all my sins past, present and future. I declare I am made righteous by the blood of Jesus by faith.

In Jesus' name, Amen.

Personal Prayer

DAY 25

RESTORATION IN THE BLOOD

(Further reading: Joel 2:25)

"As for you also, because of the blood of your covenant, I will set your prisoners free from the waterless pit.

"Return to the stronghold, you prisoners of hope. Even today I declare that I will restore double to you." Zechariah 9:11-12

PRAYER

Father God, thank you for the blood of Jesus which qualifies me for restoration according to your word. Thank you for restoration of the time that the locusts have eaten. I declare by faith that God has restored my health, wealth, joy, peace and relationships. I declare that Jesus has paid the price for my sins and He has qualified me to recover all that I have lost, and all that has been stolen.

In Jesus' name, Amen.

Personal Prayer

DAY 26

BLESSINGS IN THE BLOOD

(Further reading: I Peter 4:14, Revelation 1:3, Revelation 22:14)

"The cup of blessing which we bless, is it not the communion of the blood of Christ? The bread which we break, is it not the communion of the body of Christ?" 1 Corinthians 10:16

PRAYER

Father God, thank you for the blessing which makes me righteous through Christ Jesus. Thank you for Holy Communion through the blood and making me your son/daughter. I receive by faith every promise of the blessing.

In Jesus' name, Amen.

Personal Prayer

DAY 27

THE BLOOD GIVES ETERNAL LIFE

(Further reading: John 6:54, John 10:27-28, John 4:8, John 5:24)

"For God so loved the world that He gave His only begotten Son, that whoever believes in Him should not perish but have everlasting life." John 3:16

PRAYER

Father God, thank you for eternal life with you by faith through Christ Jesus. Thank you for the blood of Jesus which grants me access to your grace through faith. Thank you for the Holy Spirit which leads and guides me in every area of my life. Thank you for giving me life more abundantly through the blood.

In Jesus' name, Amen.

Personal Prayer

DAY 28

THE BLOOD OVERCOMES

(Further reading: I John 5:4-5)

"And they overcame him by the blood of the Lamb and by the word of their testimony, and they did not love their lives to the death." Revelation 12:11

PRAYER

Father God, thank you for the blood of Jesus that has overcome Satan and every opposition to the blessings in my life. Thank you for your word which is my testimony. Thank you for authority through the blood of Jesus to bless with my words, by faith in Christ Jesus.

In Jesus' name, Amen.

Personal Prayer

DAY 29

THE BLOOD SAVES YOU FROM WRATH

(Further reading: 2 Chronicles 32:26, I Thessalonians 1:10)

"But God demonstrates His own love toward us, in that while we were still sinners, Christ died for us.

"Much more then, having now been justified by His blood, we shall be saved from wrath through Him." Romans 5:8-9

PRAYER

Father God, thank you for the sacrifice of your Son Jesus and for your mercy and your love while I was still a sinner. Thank you for justifying me by His blood and saving me from your wrath. Thank you for reconciliation by grace through faith in Christ Jesus.

In Jesus' name, Amen.

Personal Prayer

DAY 30

THE BLOOD GIVES YOU A HEAVENLY INHERITANCE

(Further reading: I John 2:25, I Peter 1:3-4, Titus 3:7, Romans 6:23)

"And for this reason He is the Mediator of the new covenant, by means of death, for the redemption of the transgressions under the first covenant, that those who are called may receive the promise of the eternal inheritance." Hebrews 9:15

PRAYER

Father God, thank you for the blood of Jesus which assures that we have eternal life. Thank you for victory over death and the grave through Christ Jesus. I declare that by faith I am an heir to the promise.

In Jesus' name, Amen.

Personal Prayer

PRAYER OF SALVATION

Romans 10:9 says that, if you confess with your mouth the Lord Jesus and believe in your heart that God raised him from the dead, you will be saved.

Pray this:

"Father God, I know that I have sinned and have separated myself from you. Please forgive me of my sins. I accept Jesus Christ into my heart as my Lord and Savior by faith. I believe that He was crucified for my sins and was resurrected and now sits at the right hand of you, Father. I repent of my sins and I invite Christ to rule and reign in my life.

In Jesus' name I pray, Amen."